What if...
We were builders?

The Project Book for Role Play
in Early Years Settings

Published 2009 by A&C Black Publishers Limited
36 Soho Square, London W1D 3QY
www.acblack.com

ISBN 978-1-4081-1256-4

Text © Sally Featherstone 2009
Illustrations © Kerry Ingham 2009
Photographs © Justin Ingham 2009

A CIP record for this publication is available from the British Library.

Acknowledgements
Thank you to Bewley Homes plc for their help in producing
the materials in this book.

Printed in the UK by Latimer Trend & Company Ltd

This book is produced using paper that is made from wood grown in
managed, sustainable forests. It is natural, renewable and recyclable.
The logging and manufacturing processes conform to the environmental
regulations of the country of origin.

To see our full range of titles

visit **www.acblack.com/featherstone**

Contents

Introduction

What if? project books offer practitioners a wide and flexible range of resources for role play, involving children in playing out well known everyday situations and exploring those which may be less familiar. They help you make the most of an activity which all children love – pretend play and playing in a role. *What if?* project books are ideal for extending language, creativity and active learning. All materials are suitable for work in the Early Years Foundation Stage (EYFS) and Key Stage 1, with the relevant EYFS Key Early Learning Goals clearly outlined.

Each project book includes:

- A wealth of print, pictorial and photographic resources which can be used flexibly to provide children with starting points and further stimuli for expanding their play.

- A real-life photo story told in high quality photographs and short text, providing you with a resource to enrich role play and to extend children's experiences through a strong non-fiction 'story line'.

- An accompanying CD-ROM of the photo story in a Powerpoint presentation, an extended Powerpoint presentation featuring a sequence of 80 photographs with descriptive text, artwork and activity sheets. All can be projected on to an interactive whiteboard or viewed on a computer, or printed out to enhance your play.

- Practitioners' advice on how to prepare for and conduct safe and enjoyable visits.

- Resource and equipment suggestions to support learning – with an emphasis on affordability.

- Useful websites, DVDs and books, songs and rhymes, including the What if? series theme tune and song!

Key Early Learning Goals

The EYFS Early Learning Goals linked to *What if... We were builders?* and to the activities suggested are:

PERSONAL, SOCIAL AND EMOTIONAL DEVELOPMENT

- Continue to be interested, excited and motivated to learn;
- Be confident to try new activities, initiate ideas and speak in a familiar group;
- Work as part of a group or class, taking turns and sharing fairly, understanding that there needs to be agreed values and codes of behaviour for groups of people (including adults and children) to work together harmoniously;
- Dress and undress independently;
- Select and use activities and resources independently.

COMMUNICATION, LANGUAGE AND LITERACY

- Interact with others, negotiating plans and activities, taking turns in conversations;
- Enjoy listening to and using spoken and written language, and readily turn to it in their play and learning;
- Listen with enjoyment and respond to stories, songs, other music, rhymes and poems and make up their own stories, rhymes and poems;
- Extend their vocabulary, exploring the meanings and sounds of new words;
- Use language to imagine and recreate roles and experiences;
- Use talk to organise, sequence and clarify thinking, ideas, feelings and events;
- Retell narratives in the correct sequence drawing on the language patterns of stories;
- Attempt writing for various purposes, using features of different forms such as lists, stories, instructions.

PROBLEM SOLVING, REASONING AND NUMERACY

- Say and use number names in order in familiar contexts;
- Recognise numerals 1-9;
- Use everyday words to describe position.

PHYSICAL DEVELOPMENT

- Move with confidence, imagination and in safety;
- Move with control and coordination;
- Travel around, under, over and through balancing and climbing equipment;
- Show awareness of space, both of themselves and of others;
- Use a range of small and large equipment;
- Handle tools, objects, construction and malleable materials safely and with increasing control.

KNOWLEDGE AND UNDERSTANDING OF THE WORLD

- Investigate objects and materials by using all of their senses as appropriate;
- Find out about, and identify, some features of living things, objects and events they observe;
- Ask questions about why things happen and how things work;
- Build and construct with a wide range of objects, selecting appropriate resources and adapting their work where necessary;
- Select tools and techniques they need to shape, assemble and join the materials they are using;
- Find out about and identify the uses of technology in their everyday lives and use computers and programmed toys to support their learning;
- Observe, find out about, and identify, features in the place they live and the natural world.

CREATIVE DEVELOPMENT

- Recognise and explore how sounds can be changed, sing simple songs from memory, recognise repeated sounds and sound patterns and match movements to music;
- Use their imagination in art and design, music, dance, imaginative and role play and stories;
- Respond in a variety of ways to what they see, hear, smell, touch and feel;
- Express and communicate their ideas, thoughts and feelings by using a widening range of materials, suitable tools, imaginative and role play, movement, designing and making, and a variety of songs and instruments.

What if...
We were builders?

The Photo Story

How to Use the Photo Story

Read the book right through first. This will help children to understand the whole story. When you have read the story, you could go back to some of the people, activities and objects in the story. Don't try to do them all in one session, and follow the children's interests, spending more time on these.

Here are some ideas:

- Go back to the **cover** and talk about what is happening. Can the children tell you what is happening in the picture? Can they tell you the names of the vehicles and what they are for?

- Look at the **machines** in the book. Can the children name them all? Do they know what each one does? How can the builders stay safe when they are near the machines? How do the drivers know where the other builders are?

- Have a look at the page with the picture of the **site office**. Talk about what **Richard** is doing. Why does he need a computer? Look at how he stores the plans and drawings. What else is in Richard's office? Why does he need a first-aid box?

- Look at all the **signs, notices and badges** in the book. Read them together and talk about what each is for. You could make badges and signs for your own building site.

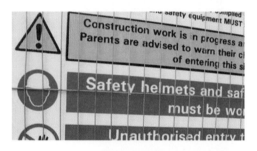

- Ask some **'thinking questions'** such as: 'What does an architect do?'; 'Can you find a picture of one in the book?'; 'How do you make cement?'; 'Why do builders wear safety equipment?'; 'How do you cut bricks?'; 'What do builders have for their dinner?'; 'Why do we need scaffolding?'; 'Why do we need to keep on building new houses?'.

- What sort of **clothes and shoes** do builders wear? Why do they need these clothes? What are the dangers on a building site?

- Could you **make a tool** like this one? What is it for? What is the next stage of building once the wooden roof has been completed?

- Talk about how you could make a **building site role play area** in your setting. What do you need?

Let's build a house!

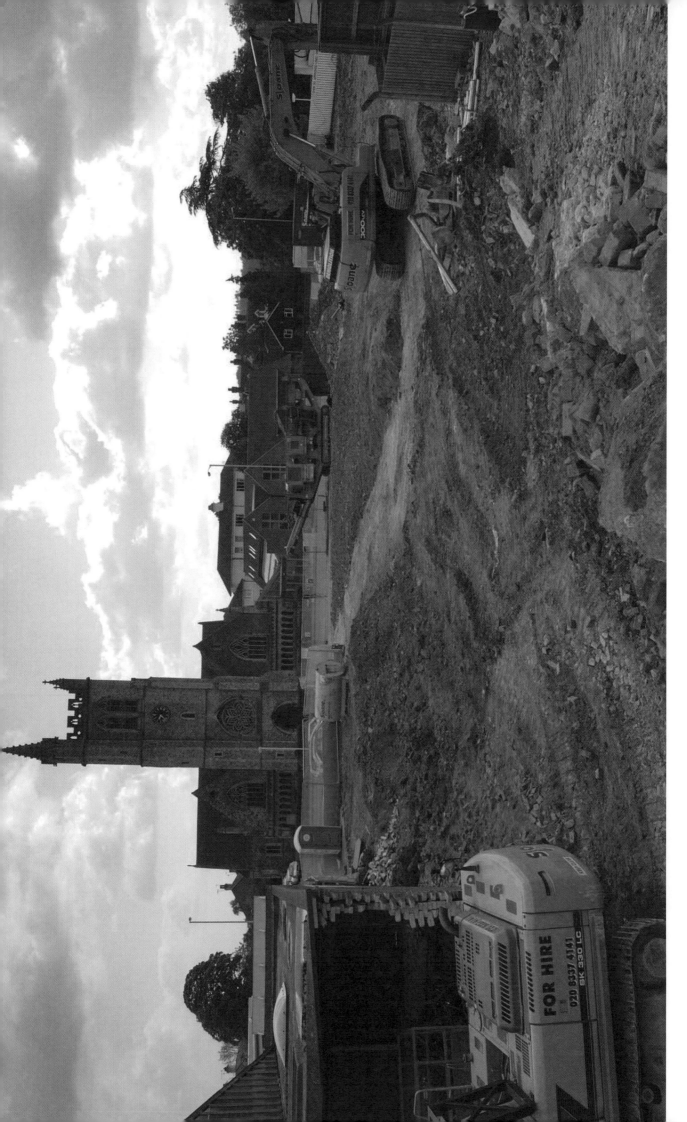

First we need to find a site and put a strong fence around it.

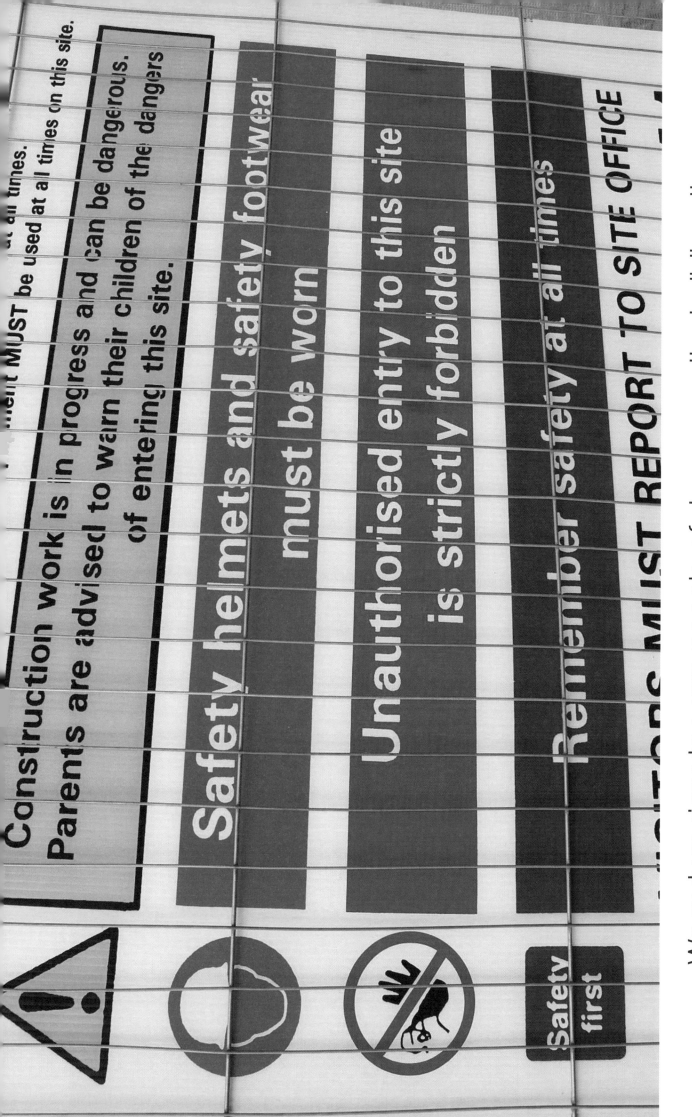

...ment MUST be used at all times.

Construction work is in progress and can be dangerous. Parents are advised to warn their children of the dangers of entering this site.

Safety helmets and safety footwear must be worn

Unauthorised entry to this site is strictly forbidden

Remember safety at all times

VISITORS MUST REPORT TO SITE OFFICE

Safety first

We put up signs to warn people of dangers on the building site.

Now we clear the site and take away all the rubbish.

We put it all in skips and take it away!

Here is the site office which has toilets and a snack room.

Richard, the site manager, is in his office.

He gives the builders the plans that the architect has drawn.

Without the plans, no one would know where to start!

A site needs lorries and trucks, so first we need to build a road.

Everyone must wear reflective jackets and safety equipment.

Sam, the tar truck driver has a TV so he can see behind the truck.

Simon digs trenches to lay cables for electricity.

Then a dumper truck covers the water pipes with gravel.

We mix water and powder from two silos to make cement.

The special mixing machine is called a Worm!

Wet cement is so heavy a forklift truck has to lift the buckets.

Bricklayers use trowels to scoop the wet cement to build walls.

A petrol grinder cuts bricks to the right size for the wall.

A string line is used to check that the wall is straight.

A spirit level is used to be sure the wall has been built properly.

When the walls are too high to reach, builders need scaffolding.

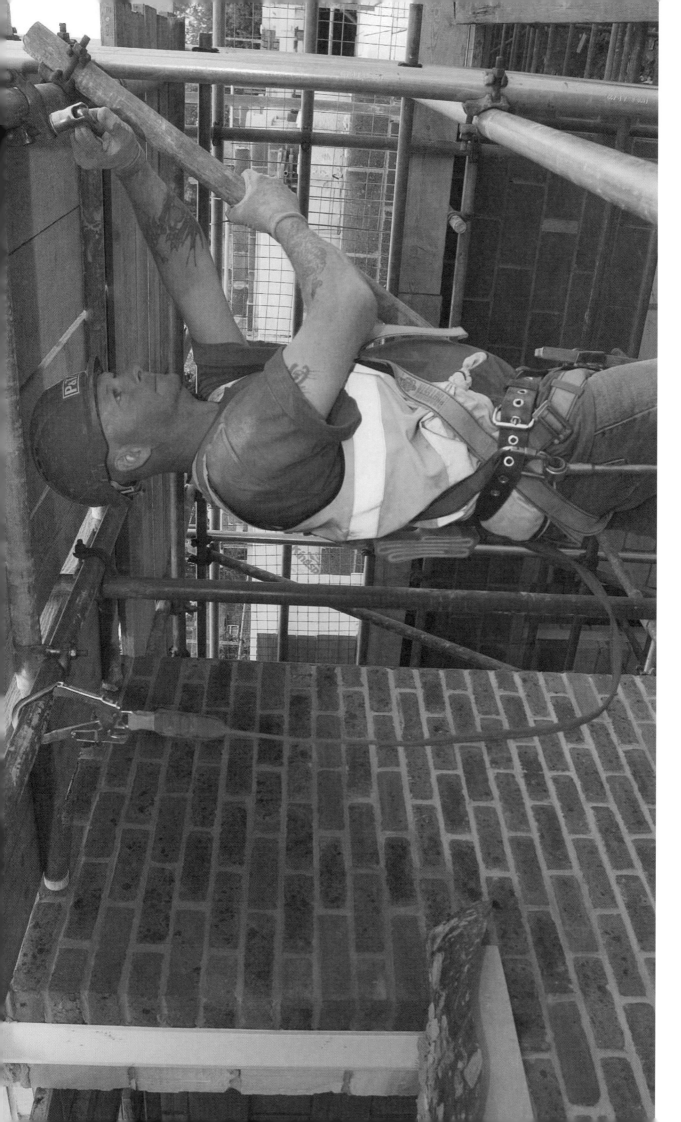

William clips himself to the high scaffolding, in case he slips.

We all need a lunch break in the builders' café!

Time for the big crane that can reach 45 metres high and lift 80 tonnes.

Only a crane can move the 2.5 tonnes concrete floor slabs!

Electricians arrive to fit electric cables for lights and power.

Carpenters saw wood for the roof beams.

They use special pencils to mark cutting lines.

Roofers cover the roof with slate tiles to keep out the rain.

Now we can fit windows and doors.

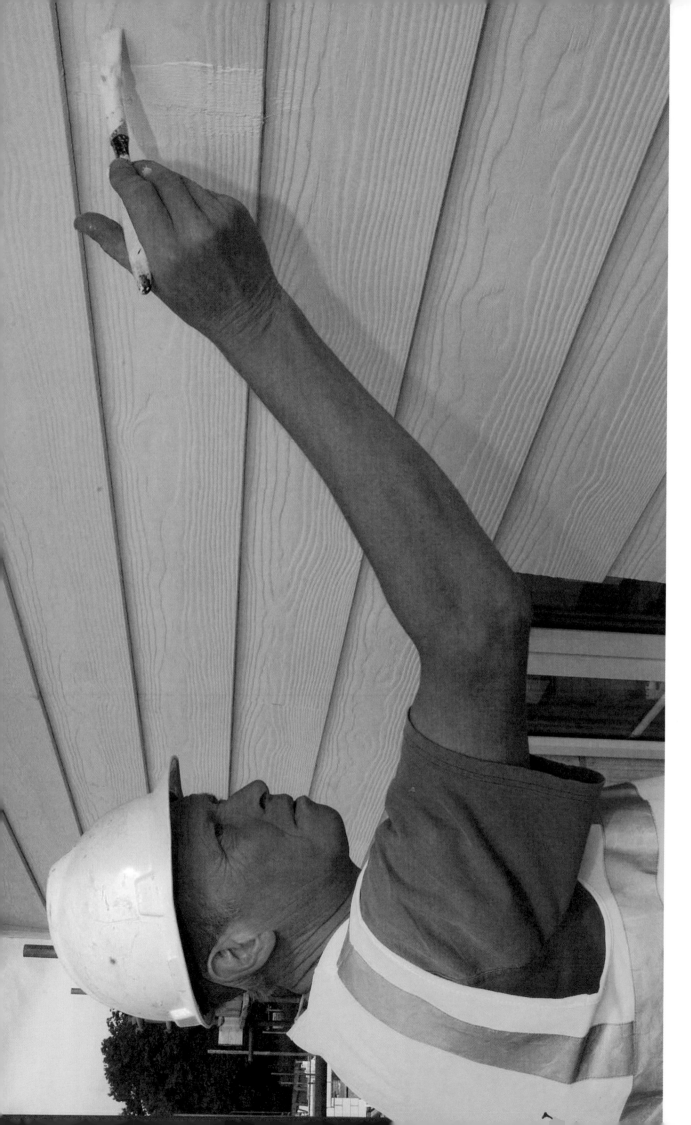

The decorators are ready to plaster, paint and tile.

The house will soon be finished and ready for sale.

What if...
We were builders?

Ideas and Activities
for Practitioners

Starter Activities

Starter activities could include:

- singing some of the songs or reading one of the themed stories;
- making one of the suggested visits;
- viewing the powerpoint presentations from the CD-ROM (printed out, on your computer or on an interactive whiteboard);
- exploring the websites with the children;
- reviewing your existing resources and adding some from the resource list;
- brainstorming with the children to find out what they already know about builders and building;
- talking about local buildings, building sites and developments;
- going for a walk and taking photographs of different sorts of buildings, concentrating on looking at how they are built;
- telling a story such as 'Bob the Builder', 'Mrs Plug the Plumber' or 'Miss Brick the Builder's Baby';
- looking in the Yellow Pages for builders and decorators, maybe one could visit you;
- looking at tools and equipment builders use, the vehicles they drive;
- printing some of the photos from the CD-ROM to make a simple display;
- displaying some nonfiction books about builders and their work.

Diggers and building sites are magnets to all children, especially boys. Make sure you talk about keeping safe.

Visits

Look around your school or setting and find the places where building is going on and where children can safely stand and watch. If you can't find a local building site, think about going to a DIY shop or builders' merchant to look at materials and tools. Perhaps one of the children has a parent or relative in the building trade, who might be prepared to come and talk to the children, or bring their tools and safety clothing. If you can't take the children out, contact a building site and ask if you can take some photos yourself which you could show to the children on a whiteboard or computer. You could also collect some adverts, leaflets, catalogues, etc. from DIY stores and mail order companies so the children can look at the tools builders use.

A visit to a building site, builders' merchant or a DIY store will need some preparation.

Before you go on a visit:

- Prepare well for the visit by knowing what you want to see or do and who you want to talk to. Always make contact with the site manager, so they know what you are planning to do, particularly when you are taking photos. Find out what they can offer;
- Prepare the children well - talk about where you are going and what you might see and what might happen (including the possibility of talking to the builders or store staff). If you are having a visitor, look at some books and some of the photos on the CD, think of some of the things you want to find out and practise the questions;
- Go on your own or with a couple of children and take photos of the building site;
- Practise being builders, plumbers and other workers. Set up a building area outside, with real bricks, planks and guttering, or use your biggest blocks;
- Look at some pictures, stories and books;
- Sing some of the songs;
- Find out if any of the children have experiences to share – have they moved to a new house? Do they know local building sites near their house?
- Find plenty of small pads and pens and clipboards for making lists, notes and plans;
- Take cameras to record what you see.

During a visit:

- Have plenty of adults around to help the children make sense of what they hear and see; keep groups as small as possible;
- Talk about the different trades involved in a building – electricians, plumbers, painters and decorators as well as bricklayers and scaffolders. Try to spot them at work on the site, or look at their specialist tools;
- Make sure the children behave well;
- Don't stay too long;
- Ask before you take photos.

When you come back:

- Talk about what you have seen, looking at any photos you have taken and anything you have brought back;
- Use the children's suggestions about making a role play setting - what you need, where to make it, how to organise it;
- Collect some hard hats, tool belts, tools, wheelbarrows and some of the other things you have seen;
- Builders need food and drink – have some sandwich boxes and shoulder bags to carry them in;
- Set up a builders' hut where you can make tea – you'll need a teapot and plenty of mugs; let the children make suggestions about where the building site will be. Maybe there could be a builders' hut indoors and a building site outside;
- Keep practising with building walls with bricks, loading barrows and carts, fixing planks and scaffolding;
- Write some thank you letters or draw some pictures!

And if the builder came to visit you:

- Talk about what they did and look at photos and pictures in books or from the CD-ROM;
- Look at some websites for some ideas;
- Sing some more songs and rhymes together as you practise what builders do.

Vocabulary

- builder
- bricklayer
- plumber
- electrician
- painter
- telephone
- architect
- plan
- house
- office block
- skyscraper
- supermarket
- lorry

- truck
- digger
- dump truck
- bricks
- slates
- paving stones
- sand
- gravel
- cement
- water
- ladder
- trowel
- brush

- bucket
- spade
- wheelbarrow
- list
- tool box
- tool belt
- spanner
- pipe
- guttering
- boots
- hard hat
- overalls
- muddy

- strong
- heavy
- lifting
- scaffolding
- fence
- gate
- sign
- keep out
- danger
- tea
- sandwich
- fruit
- site

HEALTH AND SAFETY!

Health and safety near any sort of building site or construction is really important, and children should understand why. In this case it's better for them to be a bit over-anxious than in danger!

1 When you visit a building site or look at pictures, focus on the barriers, notices and signs that keep observers **safe**.

2 Look at the way the builders wear **protective clothing**, reflective jackets, gloves and special footwear. Talk about why this might be.

3 Talk about the way the workers **look after their tools**.

4 Talk about the lorry and truck **drivers**. How do they make sure they are driving, lifting, scooping and tipping safely?

5 Talk about **safety with tools** – how do workmen keep their tools safe?

6 Look at a **first aid box** and the things it contains. Talk about what the objects are for and how they are used.

7 Make sure children know what to do if there is an **emergency**. Insist on regular fire practices and help children to learn the safety codes.

Download and print the safety on building sites leaflet
(http://www.hse.gov.uk/pubns/misc447.pdf for a free 'safety on building sites' leaflet for children)

One basic rule for children:

NEVER GO ON A BUILDING SITE!

This is because there are many hazards such as:

- **large vehicles coming from and going to the site;**
- **falling building materials;**
- **heavy machinery that can cause serious damage.**

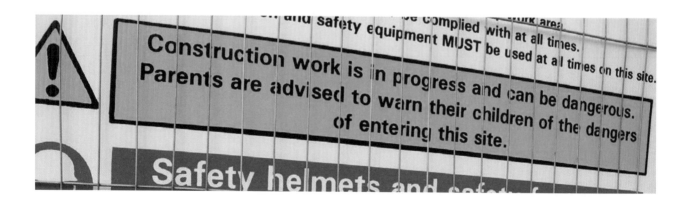

Role Play

Children love being builders, and this play particularly attracts boys. If you can have real bricks, tools, clothing etc. it's better, because children love the challenge of building and working with real things. Try to get some child-sized real tools and buy or make some tool belts. Children will have far fewer accidents with real tools as long as you teach them how to use them safely. If you haven't got access to real equipment, use big wooden bricks and the strongest play tools you can find.

Your role play setting might be:

- a **reconstruction of an experience** of a visit to a real building site, with all the things the children saw on the visit;
- a **story place** – Bob the Builder's yard, Baby Brick's house and garden, or Harvey's workshop where characters and stories from books can be replayed;
- an **imagined place** that the children have never visited, that they make with your help from the information in books, photos, video and stories or from a visiting expert.

Depending on where you start, the children will have plenty of ideas of the things they need, the place they want to play and how to organise the resources. Remember that domestic play will be a strong feature of this activity, so children will be fascinated with stacking and building, carrying things from one place to another, filling and emptying wheelbarrows and trucks, and even making tea, or having a picnic break. You could even incorporate your snack arrangements in the play setting.

Use the photos you took on a visit or those on the CD-ROM to help with the decisions about what is needed and how it could be found, made, replicated or pretended. Children are very inventive so don't restrict their creativity by trying to make things look too much like the 'real thing'. Children will often use the most surprising substitutes for real life tools, equipment or food.

Making a builders' office just inside (or outside) the door will encourage children to use telephones, note pads, computers etc to order and organise what they are doing. Offer mark making equipment and a pinboard for plans and lists. Always ask the children what they think they would like and respond to their questions, requests and ideas about the play - this way, you may get some surprises, but you will certainly get a place that the children will get involved in and understand.

You could link this role play with projects or topics on People Who Help Us, Our Community, Buildings or Construction. It could also support Science, Technology, Geography and Citizenship in Key Stage 1.

Setting up the role play

Your role play setting can be indoors or out - or even in two places:
- an office indoors and a builders' yard outside for equipment and deliveries;
- a house indoors with a phone and a builders' van outside;
- a full building site with a pop up tent for an office or a tea tent;
- an office in the toy shed;
- a builders' house indoors (for clothes, boots, sandwich box etc.) and a building site outside with another phone to call when it's time for work.

Resource Suggestions

It need not be expensive to find creative items for role play - let imagination do the work! Don't forget to ask the children what they need for their play and don't provide everything at once - start small and add things as the children need them.

Free or sometimes donated if you or the children ask:

- card for labels, badges, signs and menus
- scrap paper for plans and notes
- saucepans, kettles, mugs and kitchen implements
- boxes from washing machines and fridges (to make screens and counter tops)
- big pieces of fabric, pegs and string to make shelters and dens for offices and tea tents (old sheets work well)
- magazines and papers with pictures of buildings, tools, people

Cheap, charity or bargain shop:

- plastic and paper plates, mugs, metal teapots and sandwich boxes
- buckets and bowls
- note books, clip boards, post-its and pens
- guttering and tubes
- plastic sheets
- tool belts and tools (watch for safety)
- phones - mobiles, hands free and fixed
- rope, clips, elastic 'bungees'
- builders' trays (cement mixing trays)

Some things to include in your indoor/outdoor apparatus:

- screens and big boxes to make offices and shelters
- some lightweight tables and chairs – look for children's outdoor furniture in sales, motorway service shops and garages
- bricks of all sorts – real ones, wooden blocks, plastic bricks
- ladders, tunnels, planks and frames for scaffolding and building
- signs and adverts for safety, directions etc (e.g. STOP signs for the gate)

For the dress-up box:

- shirts for overalls – cut off the collar and shorten the sleeves – then children can wear them back to front
- child-sized plastic hard hats, boots and badges
- reflective waistcoats

To make or find:

- small world vehicles to play out the role play small size in trays of sand or gravel
- booking diaries, messages, notices, signs
- plans of buildings (download some from Google)
- signs to the site office, the kitchen 'Staff Only' etc.
- catalogues and pictures of equipment and materials

Extending the Play

- Talk about the things builders do, how they keep the site safe, how they work together to build and complete the building.
- Talk about what the foreman, the gate-keeper, the architect, the building inspector does.
- Talk about how builders clear up at the end of the day, put away their tools and make sure the site is safe and secure.
- Talk about different sorts of buildings and places where building happens – roads, motorways, bridges, flats, airports, shopping centres, houses and offices.
- Contact your local newspaper (the press department) or your Planning Department, and see if they have any photos of unusual stories about building and new local building projects.
- Set up a tea break at snack time for the builders, with 'tea' in mugs and sandwiches or toast.
- Talk about food safety on building sites, download information from the internet.
- Make a scrapbook of pictures of tools, equipment, vehicles and clothing from magazines, menus or Google images. Stick the pictures on card as an ideas book for the area.
- Join in the role play – be a visitor, an architect or the building inspector. Ask for a job to be done, or even complain!
- Set up some scenarios – a late delivery of some bricks, a bit of the building falling down, a key person missing, losing the key to the gate. Use these to talk about and work through problem solving situations.
- Do some sequencing, either with cards or photos and either talk them through or play sequencing games. Base these on building sequences: What happens first? What is under the ground? How does the water get to the tap? How do you make cement and then build a strong wall?
- Watch a video or DVD sequence of builders at work, and use it to help with introducing different scenes and situations.
- Get the children to advertise for a new plumber, site manager, tea boy etc. Write an advert, interview applicants and train the new person.

Songs and Rhymes

● **ONE BRICK, TWO BRICK - sung to 'One Potato, two Potato'**

One brick, two brick,

Three brick, four,

Five brick, six brick,

Seven brick, more!

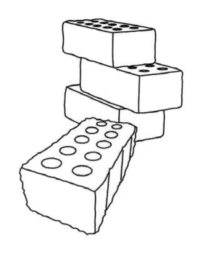

● **NOISY NAILS**

I use my hammer and five nails.

(Show 5 fingers.)

'That's too noisy', my neighbour wails!

(Raise voice.)

I'll hammer them now before it's night!

1, 2, 3, 4, 5

(Pretend to hammer.)

And to my neighbour I'll be polite!

● **RIDING IN MY VAN - rap or poem**

I have on my vest and my hard hat too!

(Touch chest and hold hand over eyes.)

They are yellow and they are new!

(Clap on 'yellow' and on 'new'.)

I'm riding in my van and taking in the view.

(Pretend to be driving.)

Maybe next time you can come too!

(Still pretend to be driving.)

● THIS IS THE HOUSE THAT WE BUILT

This is Michael who drew the plan

To give to the boss whose name was Stan

And Julie's the driver who drives the van

That carries as many bricks as it can

And Jim is the tea boy who makes the tea

To give to the builders all for free

And Karim's the bricklayer, big and strong

Who builds brick walls all day long

And this is his friend whose name is Tom

Who fixes pipes and screws them on

So we don't have a flood when the water's turned on.

And Netta's the guard who looks after the site

And her dog is Rex, who gives burglars a fright

If they come in the gate in the dark, dark night

And Jon drives a digger, a great big one

Here's his friend Charley who smiles like the sun

And makes sure all the builders have hats when they come

And strong boots for their feet, and a jacket so bright

To make sure they are safe and always in sight

And this is the carpenter, can you see

How he hammers the nails in one, two, three

To make us a house all cosy and neat

Where we can all play now it's almost complete.

Dana likes painting so she does the walls

And David paints pictures to hang in the hall

And Charlotte helps make us some curtains with stripes

While Samir cleans out all the cupboards with wipes

And brushes the floors and puts up some hooks

And fixes some planks for our TV and books

So here we all are in a lovely new home

So proud to have built it all on our own!

● DOWN BY THE BUILDING SITE

Down by the building site

Early in the morning

See the little diggers

All in a row

See the digger drivers

Turn the little handles

Brmm, brmm, toot, toot

Off we go!

● FIVE STRONG BUILDERS

Five strong builders standing by a door -

One became a bricklayer; then there were four.

Four strong builders, build a house for me -

One became a plumber, and then there were three.

Three strong builders in all their safety gear -

One became a scaffolder, and then there were two.

Two strong builders - work in rain or sun!

One became a plasterer, and then there was one.

One strong builder what could he be?

He became the tea boy and made a cup of tea!

● THE TOOLS ON THE SITE - sung to 'The Wheels on the Bus'

The hammer on the site goes BANG BANG BANG, BANG BANG BANG,

BANG BANG BANG

The hammer on the site goes BANG BANG BANG

All day long

The drill on the site goes WHIZZ WHIZZ WHIZZ, WHIZZ WHIZZ WHIZZ,

WHIZZ WHIZZ WHIZZ

The drill on the site goes WHIZZ WHIZZ WHIZZ

All day long

The chisel on the site goes CHIP CHIP CHIP, CHIP CHIP CHIP,

CHIP CHIP CHIP

The chisel on the site goes CHIP CHIP CHIP

All day long (Add other tools etc.).

● THE VISIT RHYME

Before singing this song:

As you talk with children about a planned visit, ask the children what they think they might see there. On a flip chart or dry erase board, write down the children's ideas and incorporate them into the rhyme. Point to the words as you say them. (If you're feeling especially artistic, try drawing a simple picture or symbol that younger children can read.)

Going on a visit,

Leaving right away.

If we could, we'd stay all day!

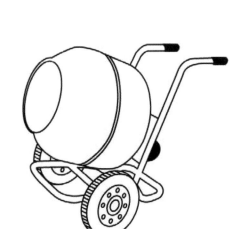

Going to the [name of destination]

What will we see?

Use your imagination;

Now tell me.

We might see a _____ and we might see a _____

And we might see a _____ and a _____ .

We might see a _____ and we might see a _____

And we might see a _____ and a _____ .

● WEAR YOUR BOOTS - sung to 'Row, Row, Row Your Boat'

Wear, wear, wear your boots,

And hard hat every day.

It's SAFETY FIRST or else dear friend,

There'll be no work or pay.

● BUILDERS' CHORES

Sing the following song while vigorously acting out jobs one might need to do while building:

This is the way we mix cement...

This is the way we lay the tiles...

This is the way we wear our goggles...

So early in the morning.

Some possible chores to perform might include: build a road, tidy up, eat our lunch, park the van, load the bricks, lay the pipes, read the plans, etc.

Books and Stories

Title (Fiction)	Author	Publisher
The Busy Builders	Jean Adamson & Gareth Adamson	Ladybird Books Ltd
Jack the Builder	Stuart J. Murphy & Michael Rex	HarperTrophy
Road Builders	B.G. Hennessy	Puffin
Bears at Work at the Building Site	Gerald Hawksley	Orchard Books
Builder Bill	Mandy Ross & Ronne Randall	Ladybird Books Ltd
Building with Dad	Carol Nevius & Bill Thomson	Benchmark Books
Peter Potts the Plumber	Margaret Ryan & Caroline Crossland	Puffin Books
Plumber	Katherine Frew	Children's Press
Harvey the Decorator	Lars Klinting	Kingfisher Books Ltd
Harvey the Carpenter	Lars Klinting	Kingfisher Books Ltd

Title (Non-Fiction)	Author	Publisher
On a Building Site	Henry Pluckrose & Teri Gower	Franklin Watts
Diggers and Cranes	Caroline Young, Chris Lyon & Teri Gower	Usborne Books
Diggers and Trucks	Felicity Brooks & Gustavo Manvall	Usborne Publishing Ltd
On the Building Site	Ian Graham	QED Publishing
We Need Plumbers	Helen Frost & Gail Saunders-Smith	Pebble Books
Building Tools	Inez Snyder	Children's Press
Big Building Site	John Deere	Dorling Kindersley Publishers Ltd
A Day with an Electrician	Mark Thomas	Children's Press
A Day with a Brick Layer	Mark Thomas	Children's Press
Tonka: Building the Skyscraper	Justine Korman-Fontes & Steven James Petruccio	Cartwheel Books
Watch Out! Builders About!	Mick Mannin & Brita Granstrom	Franklin Watts Ltd
Builder for a Day (For a Day)	Dorling Kindersley	Dorling Kindersley Publishers Ltd
A Kids' Guide to Building Forts	Tom Birdseye & Bill Klein	Roberts Rinehart Publishers
Diary of an Eco-builder	Will Anderson	Green Books

Websites and DVDs

PLEASE NOTE: The content of these sites has been checked, but the possible links from them are endless. Young children should always be supervised when using the internet to avoid any accidental clicking to undesirable sites.

Addresses

Workwear - www.gbrworkwear.com or www.workwearshop.co.uk or www.buildersequipmentshop.co.uk for safety clothing such as high visibility vests, gloves and boots

Free newspaper - www.buildersmerchantsnews.co.uk

Local merchants - www.touchlocal.com enter your postcode

RIBA - www.ribafind.org Royal Institute of British Architects
(Provides a searchable directory of members and general information.)

Building photos - www.makearchitects.com for some great photos of buildings

Schools - www.buildingcentre.co.uk and click on the bit about schools

Kidzone Nursery Buildings - www.servaccomm.co.uk for prefabricated buildings

Health and Safety - www.hse.gov.uk for Health and Safety at work

Safety leaflet - http://www.hse.gov.uk/pubns/misc447.pdf for a free 'safety on building sites' leaflet for children. www.safetycentre.co.uk/activities.html/ will lead you to a collection of links for child safety on building sites, lesson plans, and children's activities.

Builders' merchants (Jewson, Homebase, B&Q, Wickes, building supplies, kitchens, bathrooms)

Google images - new nursery buildings, nursery school, builders, electrician, plumber, bricks, pipes, guttering, drainpipes, scaffolding, digger, dumper truck, etc. Google Images 'plan' will bring up lots of plans of different buildings, which you can download or click through to the website where they appear. Or you could ring a local architect and see if they have any old copies of plans that the children could have.

DVDs

Bob the Builder

Real Life Action At The Building Site - Simon Jones

Big Machines 1 - Diggers And Dumpers - Big Machines

Ready 2 Learn - Diggers And Dumpers - Ready 2 Learn

I Love My JCB (*Includes free Child Ticket to Legoland - See T&Cs for full details)

What if...
We were builders?

What's on the CD-ROM?

The Photographs

On the CD-ROM there are two photo slideshow presentations of still photos with short text. One is the photo story featured in this book, and the other is an extended version. There are many ways to use these photos to enhance or extend your role play. Here are some ideas:

- Display the photo slideshows on a computer or on an interactive whiteboard. Use as a straight presentation, or children can revisit the whole sequence or parts of it independently as they play.

- Have a computer screen in or near the role play area with one of the slideshows running, or use as part of an interactive display of books and other equipment.

- Small groups could watch the slideshows with an adult, reading or following the text as they go along.

- Older children could use the presentations as stimulus for writing their own stories about a building site or the day in the life of a builder.

- If you are able to arrange a visit to a building site or a visit from a builder, use the photos to prepare the children, and help them to decide on questions they might ask or things they want to find out.

- Print out a photo at any size, just open the one you want and send it to your printer.

- Import the photos into a Word document if you want to make books. Just open a Word document and import the image from the CD-ROM.

- Use the photos for games: crop sections of photos for a Spot the Detail game, make small versions for a sequencing game.

- Manipulate the images to make scenes with builders in your setting, your children visiting the building site or stories of your own with characters you know.

The Artwork

Each of the *What if?* CD-ROMs contains a series of specially drawn pictures, diagrams, posters and other artwork. These include:

- vehicles;
- relevant people, their clothing and equipment;
- maps and diagrams;
- badges and signs;
- writing frames and borders for stories and pictures.

Most of the artwork appears in black line and full colour, so you can print off the pictures you need. Some ideas for using the images:

- You could make matching games, lotto, Snap etc. by printing off the pictures and laminating them. You can make the pictures any size up to A4.
- Print the pictures so children can add extra figures, their own house, speech bubbles or stories by drawing on the printed picture.
- You could also use a simple paint program on the computer to add to, adapt and manipulate the images.
- Print the dressing figures and let children stick the clothes on them – older children could name and write the different items of clothing and equipment.
- Use the images to make posters for display or to go in your role play area.
- Import the images into Word to make books and stories, using the pictures to illustrate them. Or you could print off black and white copies and photocopy them so children could colour them to make their own books.

The artwork can be used in many creative ways:
- Print them on A4 or A3 sheets for the children to talk about. Draw in extra vehicles, figures, speech bubbles etc.
- Project them on to a white sheet or a blank wall and paint round the shapes to make a background for role play or a display – depending on the size of the area available, you could create a mural or display board.
- Project them outside and draw round them with chalk (it's best to do this in a dark place or in the evening so you can see the projection). Then draw round the picture with playground chalk and let the children paint it in to make an outdoor role play area.

THE MURAL

- A facade which you can show on a computer or whiteboard, or project to create a mural in your setting.
- The builders' merchant background is an image that you can project at any size, up to the size of a whole wall. You could print this onto an OHP transparency and project it behind the role play area; you could show it on an interactive whiteboard and play in front of it; or you could project it onto a wall, sheet or shower curtain, draw round it and let the children help you paint your own background indoors or outside.
- Also available in black and white line for colouring in or to use as the template for a mural for painting.

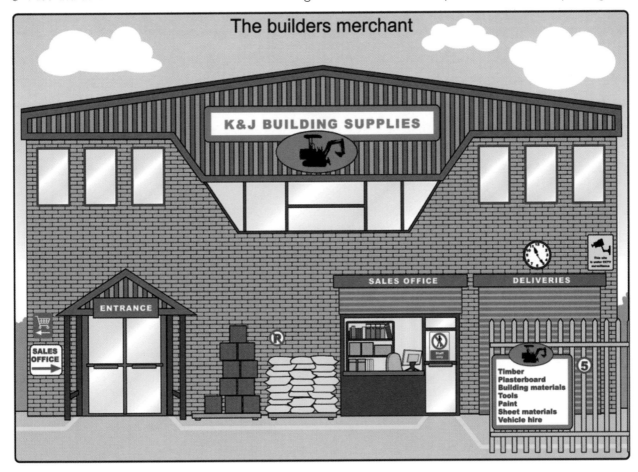

CONSTRUCTION VEHICLES

(Also available in black and white line)

A JCB loader with back hoe

A crane

A dumper truck

A cement mixer

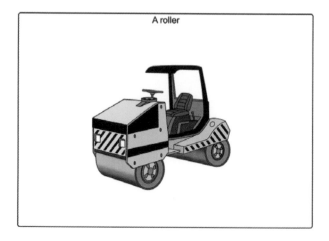

A roller

A BUILDER'S SAFETY CLOTHING

Line drawings of the items of clothing and equipment to use in flexible ways such as:

- Printing the dressing figure and letting the children stick the clothing on him.
- Older children could name and write the different items of clothing and equipment.

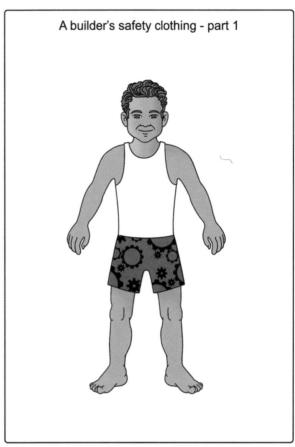

A builder's safety clothing - part 1

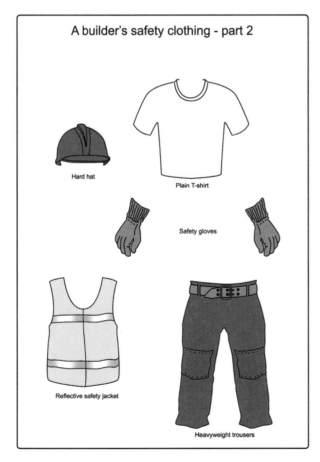

A builder's safety clothing - part 2

Hard hat

Plain T-shirt

Safety gloves

Reflective safety jacket

Heavyweight trousers

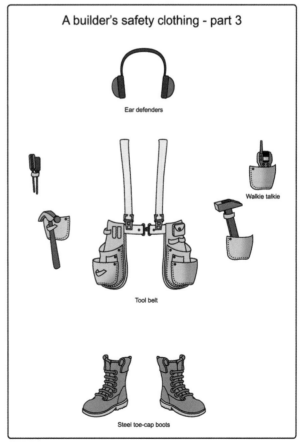

A builder's safety clothing - part 3

Ear defenders

Walkie talkie

Tool belt

Steel toe-cap boots

MAP OF A SCHOOL BUILDING SITE

- The CD-Rom has a map of a building site showing the foundations of a school, including the site office, equipment store, planned play areas and more.

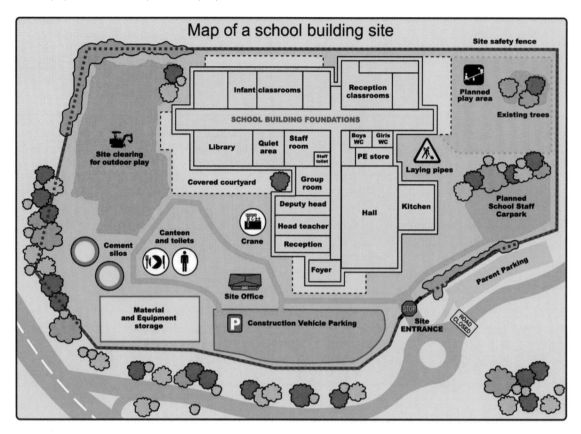

- Make your own building site with the template supplied.

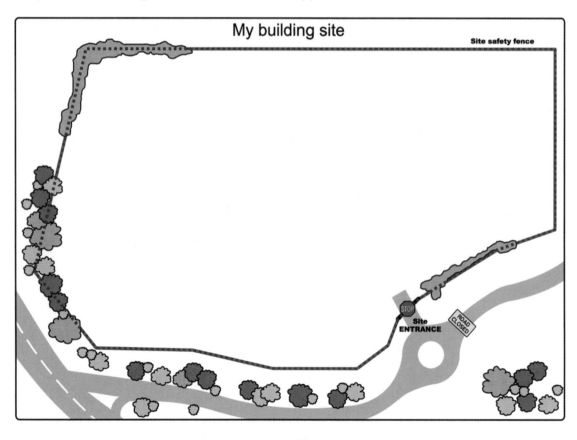

A-Z POSTER AND SAFETY SIGNS

- A poster of builders' tools and equipment, including a full set in black and white line for colouring in and a sheet of building site safety signs.

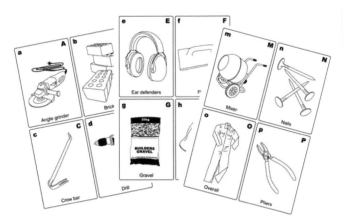

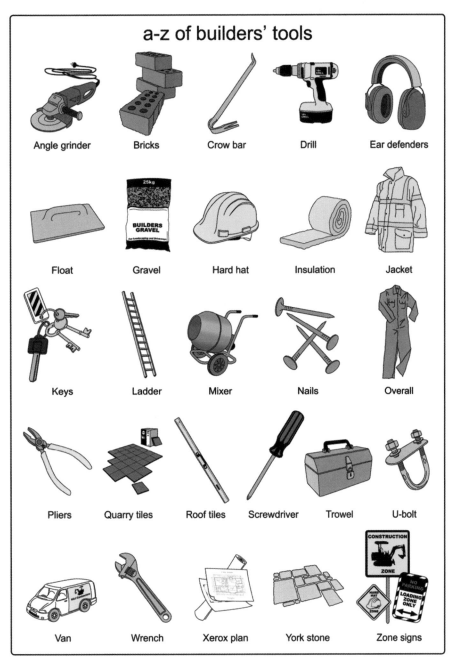

The Activity Sheets

The Activity sheets include:

- **tool box labels** with spaces for the children to do drawings or paste pictures of the items;
- **a colourful border design** for pictures and writing;
- **sequencing pictures** with a series of spaces so children can record the steps to building a home;
- **a daily timesheet** to record shifts on the building site;
- **name tags** with a range of job titles on the building site.

What's in my tool box?

Hammer	Tape measure	G clamp
Screwdriver	Chisel	Spanner
Masking tape	Notebook	Spirit level
Saw	Pencil	Sand paper

Daily Time Sheet

Employee name:

Start time	Job name	Task	End time	Total time

My name is ....and I'm building a ....

Building a home		
1. Architect plans	2. Grading the site	3. Foundations and pipes
4. Brickwork for walls	5. Roofing and tiling	6. Windows and doors
7. Flooring and electrics	8. Plumbing and decorating	9. Moving in!

Your building site name tag		
Carpenter Marcus	**Carpenter**	**Plumber**
Electrician	**Ironmonger**	**Crane operator**
Bricklayer	**Tiler**	**Decorator**
Foreman	**Architect**	**Driver**
Roofer	**Pipe fitter**	**Plasterer**